ETHICAL CONSCIOUSNESS

PAUL KILLEBREW

CANARIUM BOOKS
ANN ARBOR, STUTTGART, IOWA CITY

SPONSORED BY
THE UNIVERSITY OF MICHIGAN
CREATIVE WRITING PROGRAM

ETHICAL CONSCIOUSNESS

Canarium Books
Ann Arbor, Stuttgart, Iowa City
www.canariumbooks.org

The editors gratefully acknowledge the
University of Michigan Creative Writing Program
for editorial assistance and generous support.

Cover: David Rathman, *A Turn of the Tide*
2011, watercolor on paper, 42" x 68"
Used courtesy of the artist.

Design: Gou Dao Niao

First Edition

Printed in the United States of America

ISBN 13: 978-0-9849471-2-6

for Maggie and Elmer

CONTENTS

DISEASELESS CURE

My disease, if I
have one,
is life
in its entirety—
the white drapes,
the faceted expression,
the face
of the unerring
device, these
inscrutable tears
collecting like tulips
around a copse
of vases.
I look down
at the color
of my hands
and the color
of the floor
beneath them.
Under both
are subfloor,
studs, insulation,
dirt, civil engineering,
the perilously close
water table,
and hell.
Above, a gray
insecurity in the clouds
is as much

as we'll get
of the constantly
threatened, constantly
delayed winter,
as much
as we're likely
to learn about
the characters
in this chapter,
though we meet
eyes, smile, and
move graciously
across the tablecloth
into the arms
of the falling
rain. The cars
are freshly dented,
the houses bulging
with sheetrock
and recyclables,
the air
a vertiginous internet.
A line breaks
between clouds,
and sunlight falls
in a stripe,
scanning the barcode
of side streets
between avenues.
I stand at the edge

of my paperwork
fully accepting
the time I have
deliriously wasted
in pursuit of a more
tactful resistance
to the face
I have engorged
myself upon,
but after years
of sifting through
faulty detonators,
I've finally located
the indolent switch
and can move
in exasperation
to the chorus.

FOR DAVID PARK

The temperature is never right or wrong
here, where cinderblocks predominate
over delicately unbearable air. I take the elevator
down two floors, pass through the metal detector,
walk outside, and give to the sidewalk
what is the sidewalk's—
a species of interaction lengthening down
the open civic hallway, a spectrum of greetings
that narrows to invisibility, then opens
in the complete silence
of proximate strangers
as the implacable now
takes me back inside
the government compound, enveloped
by its pressed brown gravel and humorless
architecture, an architecture that anticipates me
like a fact anticipates being buried.
Cheap pleasantries and views of the capitol,
to be composed of nothing at all,
cold meditation on linoleum and concrete.
I drained into this building through a grid of anxiety,
I waited for the heads to turn,
to be escorted into the sunset like a sky,
for someone to stand up and insist that I,
for all my faults, am really just a compendium,
not blameless, exactly, but also not worth calculating
past the decimal. Instead, the judge
pulls his microphone through waves of trauma
and misshapes time into thin public ellipses,

and I, smeared by the ebb,
turn to face the cameras of our familiarity,
my hand on the glass and the vanishing rain.
Each step is a holograph.

ACTUALLY PRESENT

I don't remember you, but you keep coming back.
Is that what you think of me?
I've got two sick children. My little girl
has a hole in her belly
and we have to pour milk down her throat.
So much the better, make it difficult and meaningless
as when we turn into the park and hope
the conversation picks up somehow.
My heart wasn't in it, I think you knew even then,
but I wanted to rearrange thin bars of thought
into a ladder-like system of total devotion to the present
in its fabulous vanity. You were beautiful to me,
your lapel against your chin and the orange light
flinging itself from your mouth.
At the top of the hill you could see all four walls,
it was windy,
the ceremony was invested with deepening resolve,
reflection, amazement, cast out of the boredom
at the center of all things.
I walked down the middle of the bus.
I took a photograph.
I read about a town in East Texas
where a crust lowered onto all nakedness,
then dusted away with every glance.
I plugged in my computer
and looked around at the mess
as you moved
through subtle modulations of texture
from one end of the room

to the other. Something
something something, something
something something.

REALLY ISN'T

It is such
a beautiful world,
and yet
I treat
so many things
as emblematic,
as if each
teardrop on
the brim of
his lies
spoke for
a large and
shadowy theme,
like the mind
emulsifying
with its
backdrop of sleep,
black wave-shaped
cutouts in
cardboard bobbing
in asynchronous
ovals and
staggered to
the back of
the stage,
as if depth
were only a
matter of
layering planes.

UNREACHED AGREEMENT

Where everything is, exactly, now,
how it resides in a certain
field of vision
and then punches out of the air
into explosive fact, anchors
in empty cylinders.
He showed her into the living room
and felt for the buttons on his collar
while she watched him over the bridge of her nose.
Miles from tolerable,
single photographs in separate boxes
laid out in a grid,
motion and sparse
arrangement, naked
human beings
hurled into darkness
and you couldn't even look up
but who could
with the neon
twisting like an interstate
through our bodies.
No one heard me
peeling the orange.
I lived mostly as a walk
through frozen iterations
of a neighborhood,
everyone's briefly meeting faces
seeming to allude
to a future conversation

in a smoke-filled garden
draped in beads.
Theories found us
huddled in our comfortable resemblances,
scouring each change
in the melody of conversation
for a method,
a route through the atmosphere
from eyes like condemned theaters
to the adventure of pure meaning
we are sure awaits us.

EXPERIMENT

I drew
a circle
on the wall,
pressed
myself flat
against it,
and tried
to tune
the particles
in my body
to align
with the empty
spaces between
the particles
of the wall
and vice
versa, so
that the wall
and I
would become
an integrated
mesh as
I pressed
into and
eventually
through it
entirely.
The problem
was not

a lack of
gaps—
so much
of everything
is gaps,
and neither
the wall
nor my
body are
really even
all that
dense—but
ordering
the open
space that
leavens
our density
seemed to
require more
than flat
mental activity,
for me,
anyway.

SONNET

Lights turned on around you.
Now everyone has his eye.
You mind wearing a shirt?
I grasped for an order.
The painting was all blocks.
You're so good to me.
She asked him about stages.
It wasn't worth the trouble.
I ran into the store.
I left home, only later.
Police measured the streets.
Rooftops checkered the winsome night.
Outside the courthouse, they cried.
Light spiraled over the water.

THE SAME

The dominant
palette was
1961, though
the television clashed.
I sat
admiring space
rippling off
in rhythmic blurs,
clarifying certain
beliefs about
light. I am
in the human
world and not in
the human world.
The sense
of what I am
refracts off
the expressions
of those I
come up against,
objects shedding
awareness of time,
facts distorting
as they explain.
My hair had
taken on a
JFK quality
that morning,
and I had on

a nice shirt
with a button-down collar,
and I was in Nashville
standing on comfortable
hardwoods in a foyer
while commercials
for a Honda chain
poached the air
into boredom.
I worried
that conclusions
would develop
from the embarrassing
implications of
the box of cereal
composed plainly
next to the dirty
spoons on the counter.
Can they
issue forth
from the spirit,
or are they actions
no one has
any say about,
rain hitting the pavement
as children run
between the chain-link
fence and the hill?
I swayed from
room to room

in a dense
and complicated music
that drove pleasurably
though an intuitive
and incoherent math.
It was hard
not to read it,
but I knew
it was best for me
to lean against
the bank of outlets,
where a less
specific sufficiency
leaves signs
that cannot be traced
within the more
regular cone
of attention.

ON A FINGER

Here we are,
no one compared to no one,
hallucinating an agreement,
bending under the weight
of massive variations
from one insight to the next.
Can anyone hold onto the flash in the mind
of the rage in which this morning is kept?
Everyone knew,
everyone could hear
the constant slamming together of
alive and so breathless,
so flattened
against a wave of recognition
in the face of events,
paths crossing
along the edge
of a pencil,
how you strain to see
through the cracks
between your fingers.
It's over, or at least
it's dropped to such
a low level of activity
that it might as well be.
You moved closer
and for the first time
I could see the pattern.
Certainties form,

disband, and
cyclically realign
under different colors,
but each prayer
from the angle of blunt attraction
has a sender,
and every afternoon
its silhouette.

ETHICAL CONSCIOUSNESS

The shape through which
all sensations
pass changes
with such irregularity
that the whole
idea of
sympathetic vibrations
instilling each
likeness with likeness
along the spine
of disposition
seems as precarious
as your belief
in life,
how it gathers
at the edge
of each moment
and then
disappears,
blots itself out
in the rush
of perceptions
as if it
knew that it
was no longer
interesting, at least
not until
the experience
subsides and you

look around
at the tide
of conversation
you've been
steadily swimming
against without
even knowing it
though sensing
the strain of
wasted effort, words
you said but
might as well
not have,
that you
might as well
have printed on
index cards
and thrown away.
Maybe it's
the sense
of doubt—
the siblings
of every choice
collaborating in the
breaks that syncopate
the turns from
one distraction
to the next
like a standing corpse
that keeps

keeling over
zombie-like
into you—
but doubt
emulsified
with guilt
because wouldn't
a better person
have known
rather than asked
why you're
doing *this*
instead of something
else, *anything*
else, and wouldn't
anything else
have been more
meaningful to
the life force
you've gradually whittled
down to a toothpick—*this*
is the subtlety
that's become
of your founding commitment
to loving stupidly.
A pain in your stomach
crests out of
the deafening hum
of sensations,
a peak

on the read-out,
five lanes merging
into one.
Shadows of clouds
deform as they pass
over hills
like flecks of consciousness
bending along
contours of the soul.
It's as if the self
were a series of
statements
occasionally arranged
in dizzying
complexity but
mostly repeating
ten or eleven sentences
from the brief oeuvre
of a personality
that grows only
like a balloon—
never more surface,
just more tension
as the surface
spreads.
And yet
some situations
seem no more
opaque or uncompromising
than a fine mesh

that at certain
angles you can
see straight through.
Could you also
pass through
entirely, or is that
one of those
axiomatic falsehoods
upon which so
little of existence
finds any
footing and
that yet
persists? Or
maybe it actually
is true, only
more complicated
than would seem
to be necessary,
a baroque, Rube
Goldberg contraption
of multi-tiered
syllogisms and
braided epicycles
that, despite all
appearances, somehow
manages to serve
its purpose.
Or maybe it's
simple but

incredibly brutal,
a psychic episiotomy
that to experience
is to never again
be the same.
As in,
to transcend,
or, perhaps,
to be transcended.
It's summer.
No one cares
that you've learned
nothing about
how to climb the peak of
one day and
coast down
into the next,
how experience,
which was
supposed to be
not only rich
but charitable
could be preserved
in the soul,
could hover around you,
buffering and filtering
the arriving and departing
information
so that nothing
is reduced anymore

to its essence
but instead
is flavored
with the
incantatory reveries
of the coolly detached
mind. That's not
how it worked out.
Your hair
is clean and light,
the sky empty,
all protons of life
tuned and extravagant.
You occur
to yourself
as a cheerful
babble, never-
ending, "a very
gullible consciousness
provisionally existing
among inexplicable
mysteries," as James
Branch Cabell wrote
hundreds of years ago
in 1919.
Could any of this
ever happen again,
in this exact order?
Mute premonitions
glitter through

your fingernails,
cars stack up
at the exit like
words in a sentence,
the sky so
beautiful that
it seems
to be perceiving
you, your
short piano
of intuitions and
doubts, and how
dignifying is
its concern.
But do you stand there
and beam out
elementary particles
of your specific
regard like
the sun? Or do
the particles
fly inward,
condense into
unbearable truth
and disappear?
Later, as the
prow of the canoe
elbows cinematically
through the reeds,
the boathouse

slips behind
the curtain
of trees along
the point,
the hills
in the distance
layer one upon
the next—
the green
of each hill
a few inches less
vivid than the
hill in front
of it—
and the water
makes its own
claims on
the line your body
slowly traces
through this world,
nothing will be
more obvious
than the crack
in the ceiling
you've somehow
always known
yourself to be.
You see its shape
through its effects,
the turn in the air,

how your voice
pitched unexpectedly
as you read
the headlines
of a new town
through a kaleidoscope
of rain
on the windshield—
as they drop
into dark
swimming pools,
each nickel
makes a note
that is entirely
specific
not only to
its exact shape and
weight, but
also to the conditions
in which it
fell. That note
can be known
with incredible
precision. You,
on the other hand,
left for twenty years
then came back
swathed in immaculate gray
and took up
right where you

left off, though with
an unspoken awareness
that you had chosen to,
that you had made
a choice
with the quality
of actual freedom.
You fell casually
into the facts
of the air,
the balance of reflections
and sounds,
water in the evening,
purple wildflowers
spreading like a rash
on the hillside,
a boat fit snugly
in a constellation.
Day after day
you see
the unbelievable sun
as it never existed,
all description and
no sound.

PLANKS AND FRAMES

Each letter
hung on flat
undulations
and then dropped
one after another
onto the empty floor.
No one
was home,
and I didn't
know what would
happen. I saw
a spray of red
across the frosted glass,
I pasted on a look,
I waited
for the hydraulics
of enjoyment
to level off
inside the composition
of what happened—
the door disintegrates
and then your eyes
in narrow shifts
of activity.
In a geometric inclination
through the door
to the street,
flush to the edges
of ourselves,

we were a total person
with a certain tilt.
Two street lights
pulsed orange
flowers through
a dull fog.
Sheets of glass
stacked up behind
my forehead,
bending glints
from what I
saw into pure
color and dampening
voices to the frontier
of understanding.
We became a pyramid
and then flattened
to a square, down
in hungry meaning,
enough never reaching
enough. I got up
in the morning
and rubbed my eyes.
The light went
up and down
on the wall,
beautiful on
a soundtrack of cars.

MIDDLE NAME

I'm an old woman.

I wore a yellow dress to the airport so they'd see me.

I got kids, but they're grown.

I had a sensation to the side of my leg, but not the side where I already had a leg, the other side.

I stepped onto the escalator.

I drew up plans for it in my mind, where on this side it was going to be all glass, so that you could see straight out into the trees and weather.

I sit here sometimes and try to remember what the phone sounds like, and then the thermostat will click or there'll be a creak or something, and I just about die.

I had worse jobs.

When I was still practicing law I remember this guy asked me if he cut a hole in his roof if he could sue the city.

I said for what?

He said I don't know you're the lawyer.

NEUTRALITY AND PROFIT

In the hours between
modest concern and
searing disappointment,
the way you live
in the privacy of your laughter
matches the dance
of the palm fronds
in the emasculate air.
Sunset and obligation,
sunset and promise.
I mentioned you
to the floor
on a closed morning
doused in the awareness
of the long and
unsure gestation
from *could* to *is*,
when the narrowness
that leaps from
mind to mind
in the harbor of pure locality
met its desire
in a comb.
The small threads
that braid into my face
tensed in a blast
of AC. A hexagon
shifted in my mind.
There we were,

together at last,
feeding on our thoughts
as the innertubes
carried us along.
My only wish was that
the metaphor would outlast
the afternoon. But
let's face it,
it was Bud Light
and a falling market
and the hope
that possibly
turning out
of the hallway
into the next room
would bring about
a new fashion
in the sky
and populate us
like speech-filled
balloons.
Instead
the tide drew back
and I stood next to my car
and pocked out of my swimsuit
and angled back into my pants
in the corner
between the open door
and the seat,
and I receded to the point

that hovers between
pure expressions of will—
bold footsteps
claiming the hallway
in the stupid morning—
and the stupid morning itself,
the place where
care bleaches monuments
into grass
and the businessman
swallows conversation
in the lush quiet
of the living room
as he closes
the front door
at night.

TO MY ENEMIES

Blinds divide
the light into
uneven rows—
music, no—
capsules—
as the starched
mind percolates
on end times.
I do more
before 9 a.m.
than most
people do
when they die.
I listen
to myself.
I fight
the hypothetical
posed each afternoon
by the angle
of the earth,
I go up
and I go
down. Have you
ever actually
seen me,
the sun squeezing
through the tints
of the situation
that encases me

and infusing
the skin on
my face with
colors that are
a sieve to
my concerns, my
struggle? Every
second can be
criticized, all zeroes
on the luminous
beige flag
can summon
the natural outcome
of our most
casual indifferences.
The glare from
a grocery store window
tunnels through
your pupil
straight
to the back
of your mind,
casting shadows
of the enormous,
screen-filling
handshake that ends
the scene where
the technology
of society's disenchantment
startles at the sound

of dishes crashing
across the restaurant,
only to find itself
in the gaze
of racialized desire.

DELIVERIES

Does the vacuum cleaner
mind
that it's in the lake?
What am I today, the news?
Address yourself
to the side of the building
and be alone with it.
The small occasions of the world
that I can't visualize
singly, where
you're sitting, the way
the weight
of your body
regards the shapes
it imposes
on the air.
I stand up
and live anew.
It's not always clear why I'm
this thing and not
some other thing.
I didn't hear from you
for a few weeks
and began to worry,
to liken my skin
to a patch of weeds
in the rustic shoulder
arhythmically drenched
by wind

off the ends
of passing cars.
The mind rallies
in prose. Sensible.
Sensible. Sensible.
Sensible. Are you
generally happy?
Everything rained.
I feel like a video.
Moss. Seltzer.
I resist succumbing
to the core of your approach,
finding instead
that the habits of mind
that constrain you
engender a tension
far more interesting
than what you believe
are your best ideas,
ideas that
if you
indulged them completely,
the operatic reports
of your most personal arguments
would bring us all to doubt
what had so
amazed us in the first place.
I know some
particular thing.
I have experiences of

actual awareness. Today
I walked through the rain
past an orange cat on a stoop.

JUST REMARRIED

Every detail of his story is a shadow
cast from some outcropping of his love.
I withdrew from the body.
Heat found its way through the vents,
but no,
the body was outside and life
was nonspecific—breezy looks
through a magazine, thin clouds
like a lampshade, an appearance
less composed than painted.
"Come here, and turn off those birds."
A careful hour disbands under the weight
of the astonishing trees.
I held that warmth for days after we met.
I waited for you at the coast of indulgence,
a narrow cost that develops between us
when we take a knee under the medieval cell tower.
How did you break your nose?
You were watching the cat skip casually
through fits in the carpet
when the light bulb in the lamp next to you
blipped off, and the startling orange glow
of the sunset colonized your face
and sent you into an impalpable mood.
A couple of kids jumped the fence,
a volvo plunked the notes of the avenue,
the cottonwood formed a salutation on the air
and flipped against a circle
like a melon of batteries.

BLIND PREFERENCE

I looked
at the area of your face
that spasmodically adjusted
to each cough
and bump of the language
blooming from the person
of the computer. Now
replaced itself. Balcony
and impulse.
Shadowing the curb
like a bedskirt,
homelessness immense,
button to be pressed
down through the ages,
a finding of more,
California, world
enlarged, entire
comfort. Blue
metallic flowers
crinkle in the sun,
soften under clouds,
and frame themselves
in charming red skirts.
From miles away
we see
the disagreement
mounting.
There was nothing
I could do,

and I had
no interest
in doing it.
So I leaned
back into my novel,
spread out my arms
into a haze,
and slowly reeled off
name after name
for the small gaps
in this life.
I would love
just one
totally genuine
misunderstanding.
Light blue walls
soar around me
in this calm and
dangerous city
where certain voices
are so clear
through the others,
where momentary
lapses of judgment
go on for years,
and the weather
says so much
about us. You
are like a ditch
feeding itself

to the lawn,
a regular guy
making his way
through the ocean.
States are built on
promises like you.

CORNERS AND MURDERS

What would it even
mean
to be implicit?
I ran through gallons of sunlight
and the reverberating heat
of this asphalt-heavy topography,
quickly morphing
yellow polygons
clamoring on the shiny
tops of leaves
like questions,
whether the grass
is *on* the ground
or *is* the ground, whether
what you believe
can be separated from
what those beliefs
are contingent upon.
For years you've thought
you could be arrested
at any moment—
leaving a restaurant with the kids,
woken at 3 a.m.
by a flashlight—
but still you're
no more obedient
than anyone else, a bug
trapped in a
lunch sack,

miserable. And yet
the snow keeps falling.
You step onto
this particular day
like a bus, a psychic
of your own history,
listening to everything,
siphoning every disturbance,
your brain encased
in warm foam
and freshly calibrated
each morning.
A child checks
the door handles
down the long hallway
of a hotel.
What if one
opens? What if
they all do?
The mind
tumbles out of its folds
like a shirt.
You and I
have a brief conversation
in which
neither of us breathes.

THE ANTI-CANON

A single cumulous cloud
is frozen at the horizon
like the photograph
of an explosion.
Still waiting,
the prisoner behind
a slab of glasses,
a small person
who takes it,
your government and its
unrelenting intimacy.
The overweight ground
glares at you
between cloud breaks
and there is nothing
to hear under this
wrecking ball of a sun
except the phone
that endlessly rings
in plaintive yawns
like an auditory vigil
for the drying
splotches of water
on the asphalt
and the haphazard appearance
of each thing within
each other thing.
Furrows deepen
along the impulse to speak,

the present like
a disappearing statue.
Security lights spring up
in bald daylight
as a hand suddenly
grips your elbow,
a paragraph fluttering
in your eyes.
Situations catapult
past you, each
with its own
aura of sensation,
too fast to consider
one by one
like pages
in a book
of upholstery samples.
You sink down
time-shaped contours
through altitudes
of possibility,
the water
underneath you
like a disappointed
sky, the business
of your shadow
like grass clippings
in a storm.

TEACH ME TO BOX

Just simmer down, silverware,
and stay in the icebox like a good little salad.
Where do you think you're going,
elocution class? I used to admire
your poignant nose, your mouth
rippling up from your jaw
in a dipping crest that suggested
not merely disdain,
but a full and deep understanding
acquired over years of study
that led you to this moment
when you regretfully explain
precisely why you cannot love him.
Her hair was pulled back, black
with thick lines of light
shining off it in stripes
like sunlight off a record.
She held her cards in one hand
and my arm with the other.
"Stop," she said. "You don't know
what he's capable of."
Then she smeared across the floor
like Sunday by the sea. California
gossip, Connecticut cherrytree.
Bowls stacked in the kitchen
rumble back and forth,
the waiter's desperate eyes
skittering around like moths
as his winding hands flutter

into his mouth. It would give me
no end of pleasure to leave your wardrobe forever.
Instead I walk through the night
in my thick painting and hat
waiting for someone in a life vest to come along,
tie me up, and set the egg timer for years.
The yellow man lay at the bottom of the stairs,
knocked out but breathing,
and I looked at you, clutching the banister
as feathers dropped sluggishly around you.
Could anything be done with us?
Was it always going to be this unmentionable proof
trailing after each moment like a wake?
I think our faces are completely determinate.
I fell into a category and came to rely on it
like shrubs skimming the interstate,
growing impossibly among fumes.
I just wanted the police to know,
their guns drawing open the shade
as light splatters across the bedroom
and wakes the bewildered orphan.

94 COROLLA

As she came up the steps
she saw him through a window
and stopped. It was embarrassing
what I'd convinced myself would happen.
He called it a speech—
a medium-security vessel
for transporting thought across dim borders—
but nobody would know that when he started.
The days in the next room let loose
like they'd been saving up,
pounding out perfectly intelligible catastrophes
from rimless yellow words
spoken through six feet of foam rubber in Los Angeles,
natural and unhappy in a wet diaper.
Is this really what you wanted,
a square at an angle and groan-shaped capitulation?
Take it, then, and go back to your prismatic ratios.
Light reflects off the hood of a car outside onto the ceiling
and bounds from rafter to rafter as it parks.
The crowds keep moving,
and sometimes you recognize
not an exact person
but some relationship among the shapes in his appearance
or the movement of skin over his jaw as it forms words
in a conversation you could never hope to follow.
Shattered, you look down and notice
lenses embedded in the ground around you
robotically pivot toward the elevator doors in the distance
as they slide glamorously open

to reveal a swirl of water
glittering with diamonds and tears.

NOT EVEN MELODRAMA

Christ yearns for the human soul.
Entire months lacked meaning.
You waited and watched the blood
build around the button-downs
as glorious sweat cascaded from the wicks.
Then, as a lull matured,
you calmly leaned forward,
a bale of fingers hedging your face,
and said something no one
could disagree with.
Strings in the air,
embryo spectacular,
the face of empty neutrality.
Are you "like" anything from one
second to the next?
The car finds itself in the driveway
and builds into durable fact,
grooms our premises for fruition
into a modest, literal truth.
Refreshed palette, Jesus reaching his arms
through the clouds, grass integrating in silence.
I wanted to see if I could hold everything
at a certain angle
so I could know which direction
the sound would bounce from it.
The clouds invoked the ground in monochromatic excess,
lack of light to fill the colors at the erratic horizon,
then a sudden break
and dramatic gradients appear

as randomly as a helicopter spotlight
passing fence to fence over the suburbs.
I couldn't reconcile the mist of hair
climbing around your face,
your head of white paint and pragmatism
so complete, so disappointingly believable.

MISSING CAUSE

I was pulled
out of myself
through a leisurely upheaval
into a dome of worry
so comprehensive
that every
splash of blue air
was overlaid
with punctuation
and causality.
Facts on the floor,
an impossible less,
no answers for what
and all these
promises, these
door-knockers of rain,
this news
getting less
symmetrical,
news about
living and falling
living, sweeps
of flavorful meaning
in the tournament of night.
I heard bells outside,
a boat on the river,
cars crocheting
the perilous streets
that rattle the frame.

You founder
on permanence,
necessary space,
empty months
cascading through the year,
that which
comes into
the possession
of the mind.
You saw me—
you did—
across a crisp plane
in my decisions.
Then a hand
shot through
the grate
of your
terrifying disfigurement.

EXCLAMATIONS IN EARNEST

We seem to be
surrounded. We
go straight into
the undependable
air. Movies
about us, the mush
in my mouth,
how I love
to thread our hands
through narrow trees
in a snow-drenched
painting. The red line
ruined it,
or it was just the thing,
I don't know.
Green smears
on the trees
vibrated across
the windshield.
The day flaked
off the stars
in chunks.
Monday is all
Monday, air
overwhelmed into wind.
Did enough happen?
Did anything?
A day happens
inside the mind

and part of it
becomes a law,
but that's later.
For now
the indiscretion on which
rule-making accrues
just sits there,
a frightening
thingness, a small
red ball that
drags across the days
like a buoy
dividing the water
on its way out.
Some aspirations
are so cashed
of poise that
they're felt only
as a series
of bland
prohibitions.
There aren't
any windows, or
it's only windows—
all of my intentions
are genuine.
I am a genuine,
honest person,
a person who
takes care

to rest each gesture
on tufts of charm
and good humor.
You should
think of me
as yourself,
the same
incoherence of ethical imperative,
the same
dark compromises,
but with
minor adjustments—
adjustments that
you yourself
would make,
if you could—
in the direction of
general improvement,
exercising more,
never spending
too much money.
Neither of us
can help
the position
I'm in, here,
between the lamp
and the mosquito.
I intend
the cadences of my speech
to evoke the soft,

reassuring clicks
that high-quality
stereo knobs make
as they're turned.
I am here
to tell you
that you are not
dying. You are
already dead.
You are not shrinking.
You have disappeared.
Your reputation
isn't waning. You
are unknown.
You began
as a psychological telescope.
You ended as
scotch tape
on a window
sending weird
shadows
to a curtain.

THE IDEAS

Not
a better way,
but the path
to heaven
yearns through these
yellow dispositions.
Such a
beefy misguidedness,
the leaves shaking
in untold complexity,
the created
crisis sweaty
as a cholesterol
in the one and
only daylight.
Declaration.
Mirror.
Love
reaches its arms
through your skin
and pricks
the swollen ends
of your mood.
It is
a disposition
of the mind
as it intercepts
actual things
in the world.

It is the long
wait.
I close my eyes
as the car
goes through
a cable of glare
between blocks,
and when
I open them
there is
a silver brain
coming from my face
in a long stretch
like politeness,
a hand
circling in the air
again and again
describing a blizzard.
The abundance
of review and self-
righteousness.
Considering the time
before I was born
is not difficult.
I rent attention
from my wardrobe
and grew a fire escape
from lock-down
youth in the pigeony
daylight. Rain

is prosecuting
the neighborhood
as the continuously
variable angles
of the eyes
to the world
make modest corrections
to the ideas.
Privileges
abide within
privileges.
The shadow
of a telephone pole
and its wires
drops plainly
from the side
of a van
onto the street,
and the only
color coming
from the clouds
is prettier
in the reflection
of the car window
than as-is.

MUTED FLAGS

Time is filled
with constant sound
that occasionally
impresses itself
upon a clutter
of seconds,
but even then
it has nothing
on how the mind
is embossed
with arrangements
of light.
The sky
fills and empties,
the rug splashes
with delight,
and the person
who knew
without having to ask
that there are any
number of ways
to fail your family
glided up
the steps
of the courthouse
so gracefully
you almost thought
it was worth it.
But hadn't

everything
happened already?
Hadn't you already
gone back home,
dripping from sleep
and the self
that possessed you
anew? Your
mouth plopped
open, your
tongue fell
from palate to floor,
you pulled your
eyelids apart,
laid a hand
over each cheek,
and stretched
back the sides
of your face.
And waited.
It might have been
minutes, days—time,
whatever it was,
refused to concresce
into familiar outlines,
but instead
cascaded around you
in a blossoming
orange
oval.

I was incredibly pretty
with my
dark green blouse
and red scarf,
my black eyes
set against
the cool blush
of sudden attention.
No one would believe
what could happen
in my mind.
You went
from one
place to another,
but I
remained perfectly still.
I developed
a new *kind*
of movement:
with my body
frozen, my mind
subtly rearranged
salient phenomena
within the horizon
of my perceptions.
I filled the hours
with *everything*—
ubiquitous reflection,
avoidable shadow—
and listened

to pink music
in my stomach.
O the despotic
possible! It sometimes
takes me a day
to pry my hands
out of my
hair. And in
all that time,
I focus on
the line that
to me represents
what is
fundamentally acceptable.
I wave
up and down
across it
like temperature
across a thermostat.
I stand watch
for exact correlations
between objects in space
and *shapes*,
shapes that make
tenable settings
in my eyes
but that
seem always
just
out of sync.

Not the driveway,
not the afternoon,
but me,
the Friday grass.
And you?
I knew *you*
made a decision
about *something*
that day you
crawled through the airshaft
and tore the afternoon
limb from limb,
so I
gathered my knitting,
stepped decisively
through blackest
night, and clutched
the doorknob,
which came apart
in my hand, *oh no!*
At that moment
I saw
through a suddenly
clarifying blur
much of what
I now understand
to be myself.
I had *failed*.
Couldn't I have
done more

to comb through
the forms
that later
would harvest
my strange moods
into a stranger way
of looking
through the bones
in my face
at the surrounding
earth, or
would it all just
amount,
even at its most
meticulous pagination,
to an endless
cinderblock wall?
You, on the
other hand,
with your
welling esteem,
seem more like
a doorway, *well
hello there!* Yes!
Now *would* be
a perfect time
to gender identify.
I'm a beautiful
mongoose!
Could you

switch on the light?
Can you see
into my face
through the tripling
of the implied
in the apparent?
It's a wonder,
isn't it,
that you *ever*
finish talking;
for you, nothing
can exist
on its own
but instead
has to be understood
as an interval
between stars
and the pale grass
at the bottom
of a pond
stocked well past
feasible with
the vagaries
of your ambition.
And your past?
It's like a chronic disease
that occasionally flares up
and consumes you.
I feel as though
I've only known you

through a veil
of style and decades,
as a projection
of hapless striving
come to its
predictably laughable culmination,
your clean legs
arched on a low,
glass table
in an empty library,
your head listing
just slightly
to starboard
as you lean forward
in your chair
and stare
with autistic concentration
at a blank,
white wall,
a picture
of static intensity.
Nothing wanted you
to learn its
casual sky,
to come down
from the perfect,
two-inch blue band
encircling you.
A long, slow hill
masked off

the pre-horizon,
damp with the prideful
tears of a wind farm
under dozens
of divot-shaped clouds
pressed flat
against the elevation /
dew point matrix
like tufts of dough
on glass. If only
you had aspired
to notable absence,
if you had only
been willing to wait
for the paint to dry
on the walls
of your influence
before declaring
(with typically
epigraphic intensity)
all water
the stars!
and yourself
a flavor of
bombastic mysticism
whose great irony
weaves through its claim
to no irony at all.
It was raining
in the French Quarter

and a family
walked up Decatur Street
in matching yellow
ponchos.
In a wet gust,
the mother's poncho
blew up
off her body
and waved
from her neck
into the air,
her arms wheeling,
her hands
flopping around
but finding no purchase.
The father
and kids
came to her
rescue, batting
down the plastic
and finally unearthing
the mother's face
broken into
wide laughter. I like
to have the room
composed this way
not because
I ever actually
sit and appreciate
how the desk,

the chair,
and the bookshelves
balance against their
adjoining walls
and each other,
that it is so
geometrically satisfying,
but because,
in the minutes after
I've moved the furniture
to wherever
it is,
the calm and
literal present
appears negotiably
within reach.
He draws a parallel
between the destruction
of landscapes
and the deaths
of specific
human beings
not to
bluntly philosophize
the return
to dust of all
once-dust,
but instead
because certain
agents of destruction—

if they even
have agency—
are fully agnostic
about their effects,
that human life
has been plowed under
time and again
as if it were
a train station
fallen into disrepair.
For the video
I hired five
let's say "affordable"
actors and gave them
an incredibly
rudimentary script
of fifteen short,
unconnected statements,
which I asked
them to say
one after another
directly into
the camera
in a specific
emotional register,
then to go
though the statements
again in a slightly
different register,
and then again

and again until
each actor had
gone through the statements
fifteen different ways.
What they came
up with was
insane, too much
really, so
I decided to
edit the video
by taking out
any recognizable speech
and cramming everything
else together.
The result was
a jumpy collage
of mouth noise
and unconsummated
facial expressions,
which was incredibly
tedious to edit
as I'm sure
you can imagine
because it was
often unclear
exactly where
each cut should
begin and end,
how to pin down
the point

where a sound
becomes a word
rather than
something less
recognizable,
like how some
animals or insects
are indistinguishable
from their habitats
until there's
a small movement
or a shift
in the light,
and the whole
creature appears,
suddenly so obvious.
One day
after a marathon
editing session,
I left the studio
alone at 2 a.m.
and decided
to walk home.
My eyes were
barely functioning,
and it seemed
like every sound
was a human voice,
far away or
close up,

speaking to me.
I could hardly
trust my senses,
and so it
took me some
time to comprehend
what was happening
when a man
emerged from
the shadows between
two buildings
and, practically
in a whisper,
demanded my money.
I must have
looked at him
so strangely,
not, as he might
have expected, shocked
or frightened, but
as if I'd
just walked out of
a dark theater
into the daylight,
and he were
soliciting strangers
for bit parts
in the inevitable
apocalypse.
The man was

patient with me
as I worked through
the algorithm
of this new relationship;
it was several
seconds more before
I noticed the knife
he held casually
in his right hand.
I reached
for my wallet,
remembering as I
did that all I had
was a twenty,
and it was
supposed to last me
three more days
(until my next
check came in).
I hate to think
what it says about me
that it was
not until I
realized this
that I began to panic.
I took out
my wallet
and opened it
for the man
to see, and I said,

"I have twenty
dollars. Can I
split it with you?"
To me great surprise
and relief, he said,
"Alright." I said,
"The thing is,
I have to
get change.
There's a bar
two blocks up.
Is it okay
if we go there?"
The man shrugged
his shoulders,
and we started off.
When we got
to the bar,
he waited outside,
resigned, it seemed,
to the possibility
that once inside
I would
never return.
But instead I
asked Nick
the bartender
for change,
came back out,
and handed the man

a ten-dollar bill.
He grabbed it,
turned, and ran,
and I walked home,
senses and mind
hopelessly scrambled.
I can't say
I really slept
that night. I
may have, but
at most it was
a twilight
sleep, hovering
in the threshold,
not fully committed
to either room.
I imagined each
of the actors
from my video
asking me a question
that appears in
a footnote in
the Thomas Nagel
essay "Death":
"Abraham Lincoln
was taller than
Louis XIV.
But when?"
As the night
wore on and

I leaned
further through
the threshold
into sleep,
the vision became
more elaborate.
I was surrounded
by a choir
of hundreds, all
of them speaking
the question
in unison, with
exactly the same
inflections, inflections
that cycled through
a full range of
emotions—calm
sobriety, anger,
resignation, ecstasy,
and so on—
never hitting
any particular
emotional register
more than once
the entire night.
The actors remained
still as I walked
among them, approaching
each person closely
enough to hear how

his or her voice
was both enmeshed
with and distinct
from the whole,
and then I moved
back to the
exact center
of the ring
they had formed,
their sound intensifying
into a physical
pressure on all
sides of my body,
a pressure that
modulated through
the short statement
they repeated
and often growing
so strong as
they reached
"But when?" that
I thought I
would be lifted
off the ground.
Up close each
actor's voice had
sounded thin and
unremarkable, but
together they were
unexpectedly moving.

At some point
I rolled over
and noticed
light behind
the curtains, which
I opened to see
wisps of color
in a sky
that was still so
dim I couldn't
tell if the day
was cloudless
or overcast.
I asked out loud
the question
the actors
had been reciting
all night—
"Abraham Lincoln
was taller than
Louis XIV.
But when?"—
and as I did
it occurred
to me that
there was some
chance, perhaps
a very good chance,
that other people
in the world

would be speaking
the exact words
I spoke at exactly
the same time—
not all the words,
of course, but
perhaps nine
different people were
each speaking one
of the words
as I spoke
just that word,
the ten of us forming
an incidental choir
heard only by God.
As the morning
grew into itself—
cloudless, it
turned out—
and this line
of thought developed,
it seemed likely
that perhaps several
people would be
speaking the more
common words at one
time, and that
if the words were
broken down into
their phonemes,

the choir would
be both multilingual
and quite international.
I imagined a
delusional future
where all human speech
would be recorded
for the benefit
of an idiosyncratic
dictator commanding
an army of editors
whose Sisyphean task
would be to edit
each day's recordings
down to the flickering
instances of synchronization
in the populace,
the moments when
the people truly
spoke as one—
to what end
only the future
could tell.
It struck me
that to be such
a dictator, on
the smallest scale,
may well be
within reach.
For oneself,

for instance.
With the right
technology, one
could track, systematically,
the granular conceits
of one's being,
the tendency
to angle one's head
in a certain way,
patterns of conversational
pauses, as yet
unnoticed phrasal tics,
and even
the life within,
and not only
tidal cycles
of mood
and awareness,
but also the recurrence
of thin slices
of mentation
or brief emotional
possibilities, perhaps
indexed to
metabolic shifts
of neurotransmitters
and other molecular
effluvia of the mind.
To track as many
observable points

as possible
on a spreadsheet
presumably several
feet wide, to make
observations thousands
of times a day
for months on end,
and then to
sort this neptic
dataset any
number of ways—
I got very excited
about the possibilities
for a few hours;
I came up
with what I
thought was
a pretty good title,
"What is it like
to be
Thomas Nagel?",
and I even began
sketching out
the software
and equipment needed
for what felt like
an imminently marketable
conceptual project,
but then I suddenly
lost steam.

As in so many
conceptual pieces
it occurred to me
that all the meaning
I actually cared about
would be conveyed
by the description
of the project,
leaving the actual
execution to be
somewhat pointless and
probably quite boring;
it might even be
regarded as a desperate ploy
for an aura
of authenticity, an aura
in tension with
some of the project's
more troubling
undercurrents. I considered
simply faking
the results—it's not
as if anyone
checks your math
in these things—
but a fabricated aura
of authenticity
seemed *more* desperate,
not less. Moreover,
the constant surveillance

the project entailed
felt like a reaction
not only to the previous
night's mugging,
but also to
your recently successful
run for Congress.
Or, more precisely,
your sudden disappearance
as a recognizable self
during the campaign.
I suppose I
have never
come to grips
with the strange forces
that shifted the components
of your personality
and extracted
many of them
altogether, or perhaps
submerged them,
as if to protect
them from the
turbulence above,
the violent and
widening ripples
of your prominence.
These small heuristics
of personality—
exactly the kinds

of features that my
abandoned conceptual
project would have
scrupulously documented
in myself (thereby
reassuring me
that I still had them,
that I had not
myself disappeared)—
seemed like a particularly
tragic victim
of your ambition.
Bits of conduct
that you had repeated
dozens of times
a day for as long
as I'd known you
began to surface
only sporadically,
replaced by movements
and rhetorical trajectories
that seemed to have
no origin or destination
at all. It was as if
you never again
expected to slip
into the massive
diagram of everyone's
indifference. The canned
inflections dangling

from the strikingly
inanimate gap
of your mouth
followed the machine-cut
turns of the delicate
puzzle pieces
you made of every
conversation.
You wanted the light
to wash over you
from the awe
of your listeners,
stoked by your
unctuous charisma.
Press releases
were a second skin.
Most tragic of all
is that it didn't
seem to be a pose.
Your mind appeared
to be genuinely
empty. Still,
even you
had to taste
your mouth,
to feel
the realignment
of facial muscles
as you came through
curtain after curtain.

Even you
had to wonder
when the cameras
became so inescapable.
In one photograph,
the awning behind you
flops around
like an electorate
in wind freshly authorized
by the season.
You're just
turning your face
into it, the wrinkles
around your eyes
tightening into
deep pencil strokes,
the roving spotlights
locking onto your
position. You had buttoned
your suit jacket
and tugged each cuff
in turn, and your haircut
sets your face
like a table
in a catalog.
You wanted
to be noticed
but not scrutinized,
to convey integrity
so subtly and yet

so completely
that no one
would imagine
exploring further
or even asking
a single question,
which you knew
was all it would take,
like an eccentric
copyright that
automatically expires
upon inspection.
In retrospect, I
suppose I hoped
you would actually
step deeper
into the funnel
of pure ubiquity
as it mushroomed out
into the entirety
of your potential
frothing with information,
the feeling of
breath leaving your lips,
your pores contracting,
the foreground
and the background
digitizing into
dense filigree,
each keystroke

of awareness arriving
as a novel.
I wanted
to hear you
give a speech
like this:
"Friends to whom
I will always
be younger, less
sure, somewhat confused
but still promising,
I speak to you today
to reassure you:
I'm a haze
in metric daytime
living in the elbow
of a comma. Nonetheless,
my world is ordered
by levels of intensity.
A translucent drape
softens the sky, cross-
hatched exchanges insinuate
from the television,
my fingers brush
over flaked paint
on wrought iron fixtures,
a tang of stomach
acid, a smell
of burning dust
as a lamp

comes on
after months
of darkness—
it is endless.
At a certain
level of abstraction,
it can all be imagined
as a collage of shadows
and sunlight, but
you and I know
better. All
we have seen
is fifteen feet
of road, and yet
here we are,
the Treaty of Versailles."
As you wait
for your words
to sink in,
I imagine them
tumbling
back over you,
enclosing you
in the fact
that you said them,
just then,
to no one.
Or, really,
to no one
else. A crisscross

of darkness extends
from each of your
senses, projecting
a cone of absence
into the outline
of a black sky,
an emblem of its
permutations
in a column of stars
before night is lost
in prodigal dawn.

ACKNOWLEDGMENTS

I am extremely grateful to the editors at Canarium Books. Joshua Edwards, Lynn Xu, Robyn Schiff, and Nick Twemlow have made the press's first five years ones of kindness, grace, and brilliance. I am lucky to work with them and lucky to be in the company of the press's other incredible authors.

I am grateful to Lauren Clark and Claire Skinner, at the University of Michigan MFA Program in Creative Writing, who proofread this manuscript.

Thank you Travis Nichols, Mark Molloy, Maggie Jackson, and (again) Joshua Edwards for your close readings of and suggestions for these poems.

Thank you to the editors of the following publications, where some of the poems previously appeared, sometimes in a different form: *Aufgabe*, *Better: Culture and Lit*, *The Broken Plate*, *Catch Up*, *Court Green*, *Harp & Altar*, *Poets Off Poetry*, *Poor Claudia*, and *Starting Today: 100 Poems for Obama's First 100 Days*.

"Muted Flags" owes a sizable debt to David Gatten, who allowed me to appropriate his mugging experiences for the poem. David is a person of total humanity, and he has negotiated with men who were mugging him twice, both times getting to know the men surprisingly well—one walked him home and told him where he worked, and the other showed him his driver's license, said "Show me some love!", and gave him a hug.

Finally, I feel hugely indebted to the poetry community in New Orleans, where I lived from September 2008 to December 2012 and where all of these poems were written. The incredibly talented poets there generously offered me readings and invitations to their poetry classes at arts high schools, universities, and even Orleans Parish Prison, and their support and encouragement has meant a lot to me. Thank you Adam Atkinson, Nik De Dominic, Melissa Dickey, Ben Kopel, Brad Richard, Andy Stallings, Kim Vodicka, Engram Wilkinson, and Andy Young. Thank you also to Anne Gisleson and Nate Martin, brilliant writers and tireless supporters of New Orleans's young literary community.

Paul Killebrew was born in 1978 in Nashville, Tennessee. From 2008 to 2012 he served as a staff attorney at Innocence Project New Orleans. His first full-length collection of poems, *Flowers*, was published by Canarium Books in 2010. He currently resides in Maryland with his wife and son.